SPACE!

MARS

Marshall Cavendish Benchmark
99 White Plains Road
Tarrytown, New York 10591
www.marshallcavendish.us

Library of Congress Cataloging-in-Publication Data

Capaccio, George.
  Mars / by George Capaccio.
    p. cm. — (Space!)
  Summary: "Describes Mars, including its history, its composition, and its role in the
Solar System"—Provided by publisher.
  Includes bibliographical references and index.
  ISBN 978-07614-4247-9
  1. Mars (Planet)—Juvenile literature. I. Title.
  QB641.C352 2010
  523.43—dc22
  2008037280

Editor: Karen Ang
Publisher: Michelle Bisson
Art Director: Anahid Hamparian
Series design by Daniel Roode
Production by nSight, Inc.

Front cover: A computer illustration of Mars
Title page: A computer illustration of a rover exploring the surface of Mars.
Photo research by Candlepants, Inc.
Front cover: Antonio M. Rosario / Getty Images
The photographs in this book are used by permission and through the courtesy of:
NASA: JPL-Caltech, 1, 54; JPL/University of Arizona, 20; NSSCD, 21, 56. Super Stock: Pixtal,
4, 5, 11; Digital Visions Ltd., 6, 14, 15. Photo Researchers Inc.: John Chumack, 12; NASA/
JPL/Arizona State University, 21; David A. Hardy, 24, 25; Royal Astronomical Society, 28.
AP Images: NASA/JPL, 17; European Space Agency, 19; NASA/JPL/Malin Space Science
Systems, 23, 57; 38; NASA, 42, 47; NASA Jet Propulsion Laboratory, 44, 45, 50, 52; Doug
Mills, 46. Getty Images: D'Arco Editori, 22; Space Frontiers, 59. The Bridgeman Art
Library: Nationalgalerie, SMPK, Berlin, Germany, 26; Private Collection, 29. The Image
Works: Mary Evans Picture Library, 30, 33; NASA/SSPL, 40. A. Tayfun Oner: 36.
Printed in Malaysia
123456

CONTENTS

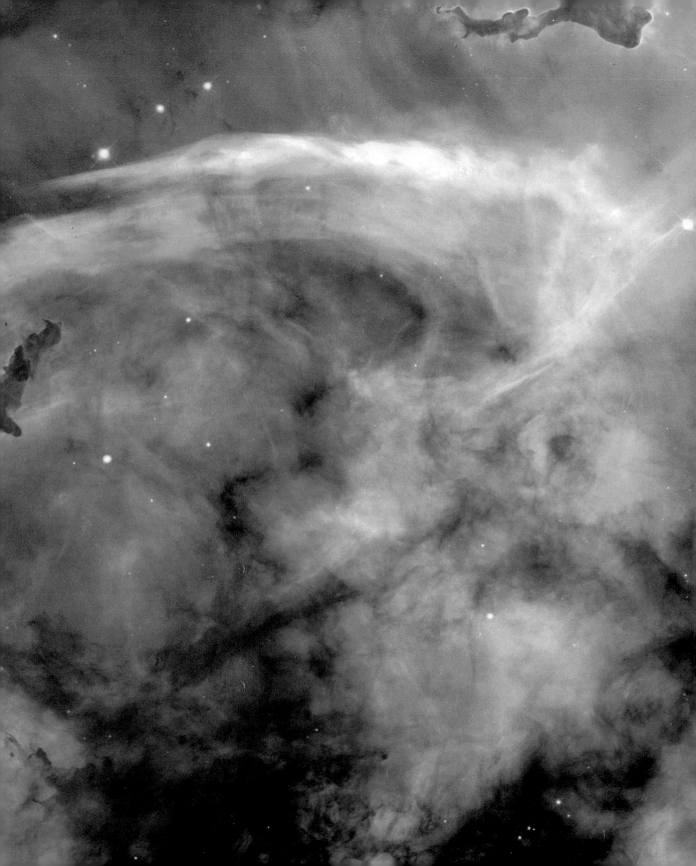

1

THE FORMATION OF OUR SOLAR SYSTEM

All of the planets are about the same age. They formed roughly 4.5 billion years ago as part of our Solar System. So how did the Solar System get started? Most scientists would agree that a huge cloud of dust grains and gas molecules that spread for millions of miles in space was the seedbed from which the Solar System grew. As the dust cloud grew smaller, the force of gravity caused particles in the center of the cloud to interact more violently as they moved closer to each other. Temperatures in the center of the cloud became so hot that hydrogen **atoms** began to fuse, or stick together. These reactions produced heat and light. The center of the cloud had become a star—the Sun.

The stars and planets formed from giant clouds of gas and dust in outer space.

As the Solar System began to form, the dust cloud spun faster and faster. Circulating dust grains and gas molecules began to merge into larger objects. Random collisions between these objects kept increasing the objects' size until, after millions of years, whole planets began to take shape.

There are eight major planets in our Solar System. These include the four **terrestrial** planets—Mercury, Venus, Earth, and Mars—and the four gas giants, which are Jupiter, Saturn, Uranus, and Neptune. Pluto used to be considered a planet, but because of its small size it is now classified as a dwarf planet. Besides the planets, there are dozens of moons and numerous asteroids, comets, and meteoroids moving through our Solar System.

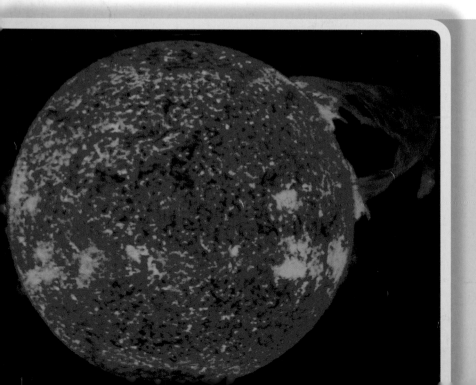

The Sun is the center of our universe, around which all planets orbit. Its light and heat determine many of the physical characteristics of the planets.

ASTEROIDS, COMETS, AND METEOROIDS

Asteroids are ancient rocks leftover from the formation of the Solar System. Most asteroids orbit the Sun in a region between Mars and Jupiter. Some of the largest known asteroids are more than 300 miles (482 kilometers) across. The smallest known asteroids are less than 1 mile (1.6 km) across. Scientists think the two moons of Mars may be asteroids that were pulled into the planet's gravitational field.

Comets are icy bodies that form in the outer edges of the Solar System. A comet has a small solid center made of ice, frozen gases, rock, and dust. The center is typically less than a few miles across. When a comet approaches the Sun, some of its surface ice melts, creating a long, streaming tail of gas and dust.

Most meteoroids probably come from within our Solar System. They are made of iron or stone or a mixture of both materials. Meteoroids that enter Earth's atmosphere become meteors, which are often called "shooting stars." If meteors reach the surface of Earth without burning up, they are called meteorites. Most are very small, but a few large ones weighing more than 50 tons (45 tonnes) have landed on Earth in the past. Sixteen meteorites found in Antarctica are known to have come from Mars.

THE GAS GIANTS

Four of the eight major planets in our Solar Systems are gas giants. They get this name because they are the four largest planets and are mostly made up of gases. Jupiter is the largest planet in our Solar System with a diameter more than eleven times the diameter of Earth. This king of planets is one big ball of hot gas. Some scientists think that Jupiter has a very small solid core, or center, while others believe that the heat and pressure on the planet forms a liquid core. Either way, scientists are pretty sure that gases, such as hydrogen, helium, and ammonia, swiftly swirl around the core, forming the planet's **atmosphere**.

Saturn is the second-largest planet in our Solar System. Like Jupiter, it consists of extremely hot gases such as hydrogen, helium, and methane. Saturn's atmospheric pressure, like Jupiter's, is so strong it would easily crush any space vehicle that passed through the planet's cloud cover. It also compresses the planet's various gases into liquids. As a result, Saturn has no hard, solid surface.

Uranus is the third-largest planet. Its blue-green color is the result of methane gas reacting with sunlight. Like Jupiter and Saturn, Uranus is not the sort of place that humans can safely visit. The atmosphere is thick and poisonous. Even though it is known as a gas giant, Uranus is also called an ice giant. This is

Of the eight main planets in our Solar System, the four closest to the Sun—Mercury, Venus, Earth, and Mars—are the terrestrial, or land, planets. Jupiter, Saturn, Uranus, and Neptune are considered gas giants. Pluto, which was once considered a main planet alongside the others, is now known as a dwarf planet.

because it is so far way from the Sun that all water and gases—such as ammonia and methane—are frozen solid.

Like Uranus, Neptune is both a gas giant and an ice giant. This fourth-largest planet gets its bluish color from the methane gas in its atmosphere. Unlike Uranus, however, scientists believe that Neptune generates its own heat from within. They think that the planet may have a **molten** and rocky core that is surrounded by a mixture of frozen water, hydrogen, helium, water, methane, and liquid ammonia.

THE TERRESTRIAL PLANETS

The four terrestrial planets—Mercury, Venus, Earth, and Mars—are closest to the Sun. Metals and rocks make up most of these planets. ("Terrestrial" refers to something made of rock or something that is land-dwelling.) Mercury is the smallest major planet and is the closest to the Sun. You might think that Mercury's climate is always blistering hot. In reality, the difference between the planet's daytime and nighttime temperatures can be greater than 1000 degrees Fahrenheit (538 degrees Celsius). This is because Mercury's atmosphere is so thin it retains, or keeps, very little of the Sun's heat during the evenings.

Mercury is hot, but Venus, the second planet from the Sun, is actually hotter. In fact, it is the hottest planet in the Solar System. The heat is so extreme it would melt zinc, which is a metal used in United States pennies and is very hard to melt. On Venus, thick clouds trap the sunlight, and temperatures can reach 900 degrees Fahrenheit (482 degrees C). Venus is our closest neighbor and after the Moon, the brightest object in the night sky. But Venus's clouds prevent direct observation of the planet's surface. However, scientists have used radar to detect deep craters and canyons in its rocky surface.

Earth is the fifth-largest planet in the Solar System and the only one where life is known to exist. Unlike every other planet, Earth has an almost ideal set of conditions for living things to grow and thrive. The distance from the Sun combined with the tilt of Earth's **axis** gives us changing seasons and a moderate range of climates. We have oceans, lakes, rivers, and streams, and many different types of environments. The rocky land surface of the planet gives us places to live. Our atmosphere provides a breathable mixture of gases and offers protection from the Sun's strong rays. The atmosphere also

Though Mars and Earth share some common features, they still have very different characteristics, such as temperature ranges and chemical makeup.

retains enough of the Sun's heat to keep the nights from getting unbearably cold in most parts of the world.

Of all the planets in the Solar System, Mars is most like our own planet. One Martian day, called a sol, is a little more than twenty-four hours long. Even the tilt of its axis is similar to Earth's. As a result, Mars enjoys distinct seasonal changes. There is even water on Mars in the form of ice, frost, fog, and clouds. Like Earth, Mars has polar ice caps, clearly visible in photos taken by orbiting spacecraft.

This photograph was taken in 2007 while viewing Mars through a very strong telescope. At the time, Mars was in opposition with Earth and the Sun, making it one of the brightest objects in the sky.

SEEING MARS

About every two years, the orbits of Mars and Earth bring the planets into opposition. When that happens, Earth is midway between Mars and the Sun, and together these three bodies line up like beads on a string. However, about every sixteen years, Mars comes close to the Sun. At these times, when Mars and Earth are on the same side of the Sun, Mars is one of the brightest objects in the night sky. Only the Sun, Earth's Moon, and the planet Venus are brighter.

HOW DO EARTH AND MARS COMPARE?

	MARS	EARTH
DIAMETER	About 4,218 miles (6,792 km)	About 7,926 miles (12,753 km)
DISTANCE FROM SUN	About 142 million miles (228 million km) but the distance varies since Mars has an elliptical orbit	About 93 million miles (150 million km).
ONE DAY	24 hours, 37 minutes (a Martian sol)	24 hours
ONE YEAR	686.98 Earth days (about 670 Mars days)	365 days
AVERAGE PLANET-WIDE TEMPERATURE	About −67 degrees Fahrenheit (−55 degrees C)	47.3 degrees Fahrenheit (8.5 degrees Celsius) over land
NUMBER OF MOONS	Two (Phobos and Deimos)	One
GRAVITY	About 38 percent of Earth's gravity	
ATMOSPHERE	About 95.3 percent carbon dioxide and 0.15 percent oxygen and small amounts of other gases. Atmosphere is much thinner than Earth's.	About 76 percent nitrogen, 21 percent oxygen, and small amounts of Argon, carbon dioxide, and neon.
MAGNETIC FIELD	Mars's weak magnetic field allows strong exposure to solar winds and radiation from the Sun and outside the Solar System.	Strong enough to protect Earth from the solar wind and some forms of radiation.
WATER	No liquid water has been found on the surface, but Mars has ice, frost, fog, and clouds. There may be underground water sources.	Earth has plenty of water.
LIFE	No life has been found on Mars. If it exists, it is probably in the form of microbes, or tiny microorganisms.	Earth has abundant and varied life-forms.

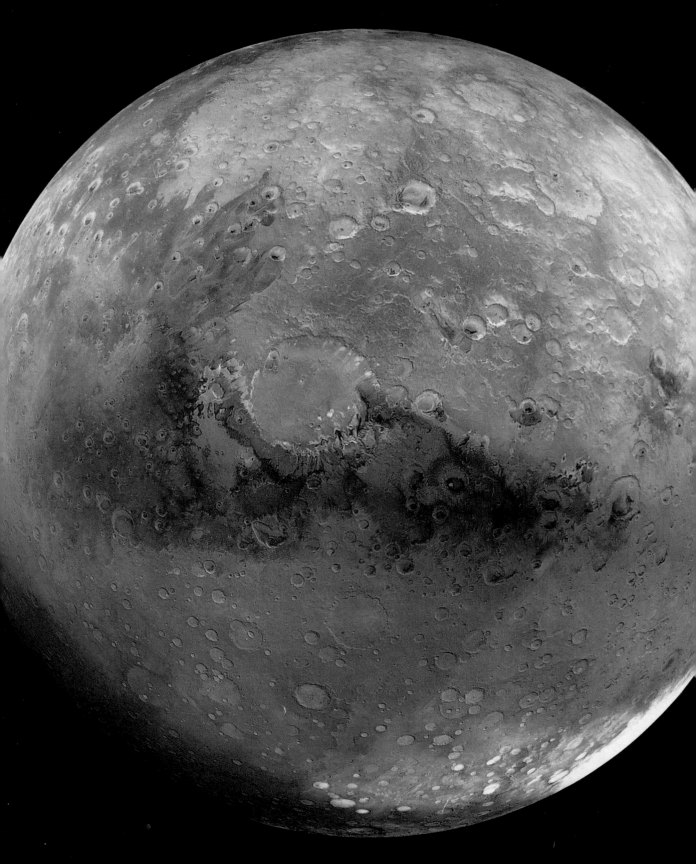

2

STRUCTURE AND PHYSICAL FEATURES OF MARS

Astronomers once believed that Mars was the home of an advanced civilization. Through telescopes they found what they thought was evidence of irrigation canals, which are used to direct water. These scientists then concluded that people from Mars, or Martians, had turned their deserts into lush orchards and farmlands. Some observers even feared that one day a dangerous dry spell on Mars would force Martians to colonize Earth in order to preserve their way of life. Not all scientists

Early observations of Mars led astronomers to believe that alien life existed on the planet. Even today, scientists continue to consider the possibility of life there.

agreed with those who claimed that intelligent beings lived on Mars. They argued that the so-called canals were actually optical illusions. These scientists said that people who saw canals on the Martian surface were connecting light and dark areas into straight lines. Their eyes were playing tricks on them.

NO PLACE FOR HUMANS

The question of whether there is or ever was life on Mars remains unanswered to this day. Mars may be Earth-like in many ways but it is not the sort of place you would want to visit unless you had adequate protection. Even then, you might not survive the planet's harsh environment. Thanks to a series of unmanned space missions to Mars, we now know that the planet is not suitable for humans. The atmosphere consists mostly of carbon dioxide, and humans need oxygen to survive. Low atmospheric pressure causes liquids to boil quickly. The atmospheric pressure on Mars is so low that without a pressurized space suit, an astronaut on Mars would not be able to keep his or her blood from boiling away. As if that were not bad enough, the Martian atmosphere offers no protection from the Sun's ultraviolet radiation. On Earth the naturally occurring ozone layer shields us from this energy. But because Mars lacks a dense atmosphere, ultraviolet light floods the planet's surface, making surface life impossible.

The thinness of the Martian atmosphere allows most of the Sun's energy to escape into space. Daytime summer temperatures on Mars can average about 50 degrees Fahrenheit (10 degrees C). But at night, the temperature can plunge below -110 degrees Fahrenheit (-78 degrees C). At the planet's poles the temperature can drop to -220 degrees Fahrenheit (-140 degrees C).

Robotic vehicles called rovers have explored the Martian surface and sent back detailed color photos of what their cameras saw. Some parts of Mars look like the American Southwest. Only on Mars there are no cacti or sagebrush plants. But there are plenty of rocks of all sizes. They are as old as the Solar System and may contain clues about the planet's distant past. The rocks rest on clay soil that has a lot of iron. The iron has rusted, giving Mars its characteristic reddish brown color. While our sky is blue, the Martian sky is pinkish. This is because swirling dust storms toss particles of the soil into the atmosphere.

Images sent back to Earth from the *Pathfinder* rover show that land features on Mars resemble some parts of Earth.

MARS IN CLOSE UP

Not too long ago, scientists thought of Mars as a cold, dead planet. That view has changed as rovers and other spacecraft have given us a much closer look. Martian geography is a lot more complex and interesting than people once thought. Mars has shifting, pinkish sand dunes, plunging canyons, huge craters, polar ice caps, and towering volcanoes. Winds can gust up to 100 miles (161 km) per hour and faster. Violent dust storms periodically cover the entire planet.

The northern hemisphere is mostly flat lowland with very few craters. In contrast, the southern hemisphere is more mountainous and has many craters. The darker- and lighter-colored regions of the planet, which once baffled scientists, are the result of different types of surfaces. Layers of bright dust reflect the sunlight, so they appear lighter, while uncovered rocky areas look darker.

WATER ON MARS

There is convincing evidence that large amounts of water once flowed on Mars. Markings on the surface of the planet appear to be dried up riverbeds. The way rocks are placed also suggests that catastrophic floods once surged across the surface.

So far, most of the water found on Mars is locked up as ice at the planet's north pole. The southern ice cap is mostly frozen carbon dioxide. As seasons change on Mars, the polar ice fields alternately melt and freeze. These changes affect the planet's weather and climate.

Scientists suspect that Mars even had lakes and oceans. A three-dimensional map created by the *Mars Global Surveyor*, an orbiting spacecraft, shows an enormous flat plain with what appears to be a shoreline similar to shorelines on Earth. Because Mars has a freezing cold climate, it is not likely that a lot of liquid water will ever be found. However, in 2000, a NASA (National Aeronautics and Space Administration) spacecraft spotted something spilling down the sides of the Nirgal Vallis, which is a 250-mile-long valley. A possible explanation is that water from underground sources is able to well up in certain places on Mars.

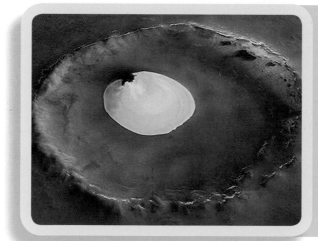

A European Space Agency spacecraft photographed this image of ice on the floor of a crater near the north pole of Mars.

SPECTACULAR NATURAL WONDERS

Mars has some pretty amazing-looking places. The physical features of Mars tend to be super-sized and are among the most outstanding in our Solar System. Volcanic mountains on Mars, though inactive, are many times larger than volcanoes found on Earth. Olympus Mons, for instance, is the highest peak in the Solar System. This Martian peak is three times higher than Mount Everest—which is 29,029 feet (8,484 meters) high—and has a base that is about as big as the state of Arizona.

Scientists think that the carved-out patterns in this gully may be proof that water once flowed across the surface of Mars.

Mars also has unbeatable canyons. Valles Marineris makes the Grand Canyon look small by comparison. Valles Marineris is a network of canyons that lies to the south of the Martian equator. It is about 3,000 miles (4,827 km) long and would stretch across the entire United States. The main canyon is 420 miles (676 km) wide. The deepest parts reach a depth of 4.2 miles (6.7 km), which is many times deeper than the Grand Canyon.

The largest sand dune field in the Solar System is near the northern polar ice cap of Mars. The dunes surround the north pole and sometimes mix with snow blowing in the region.

The western hemisphere of Mars features a broad plateau called Tharsis. It is bigger than all of Europe and contains most of the volcanoes on Mars.

Billions of years ago, meteorites and asteroids crashed into Mars, covering the planet with craters. Hellas Basin is the largest of these impact craters. If it were located on Earth, it would cover half of the United States.

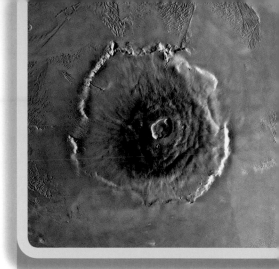

This view of Olympus Mons is a combination of images collected in 1978 by the *Viking* spacecraft.

Scientists combined information collected by satellites to create this three-dimensional image of Valles Marineris, the largest canyon system on Mars.

In the southern highlands of Mars, orbiting spacecraft have photographed a number of valleys. If flowing water carved out these valleys, then the Martian climate must have been much warmer in the past. The planet would also have needed a thicker atmosphere to keep the water from evaporating.

INSIDE MARS

Scientists think Mars has a core that is mostly molten iron or a blend of iron and sulfur. Long ago, this core was extremely hot. Like Earth's core, it generated a magnetic field that surrounded the planet. As the Martian core cooled, the magnetic field gradually weakened. It is practically all gone now. A **mantle** of different kinds of minerals surrounds the core. The Martian crust, which lies on top of the mantle, is mostly basalt. This hard black volcanic rock also covers more than half of Earth's surface. On Mars, as on Earth, the crust was formed from the melting of the upper mantle. The unique features of the Martian mantle are due to volcanic activity, erosion (the wearing away of materials), and the impact of meteorites and asteroids.

The planet's molten iron core is surrounded by layers made up of a variety of elements and rocks.

PHOBOS AND DEIMOS: THE MOONS OF MARS

Mars has two moons, and their names are Phobos and Deimos. Because of their odd shape, some astronomers have compared them to potatoes. Both moons are made of rock and ice and are very small, as far as moons go. They are actually asteroids that strayed too close to the planet's gravitational field. Phobos is about 13 miles (21 km) across at its widest point. It orbits Mars once every seven hours and thirty-nine minutes. By contrast, our Moon takes about twenty-seven days to orbit Earth. Phobos's orbit is slowly shrinking. Astronomers estimate that in about 50 million years, Phobos will either crash into Mars or break into pieces from the force of the planet's gravity.

Deimos is even smaller than Phobos. With a width of about 8 miles (13 km), this moon is one of the smallest bodies in the entire Solar System. Deimos completes one orbit every thirty hours and eighteen minutes. Scientists think it may be possible to use Deimos as a landing site for future missions to Mars. Manned missions might even store supplies and communication equipment on Deimos for base camps on Mars.

This image of Phobos was taken in 2003 by the *Mars Global Surveyor*.

3

MARS THROUGH THE AGES

Centuries before the invention of telescopes, astronomers noticed that most celestial bodies seemed to stay in one place. However, they counted five objects that were different. Not only did they shine with a steady light, but they also changed their positions during the course of a year. Ancient Greek observers called these mysterious objects "wandering stars." One of these objects seemed to have a strange reddish glow. It might have reminded people of the color of blood.

In time, this planet became connected in people's minds with war and violence. In the Babylonian and Sumerian cultures of ancient Mesopotamia—where present-day Iraq is located—

From early descriptions more than one hundred years ago (upper right) to present-day satellite imagery (center), the way scientists observe and understand Mars has changed through the years. Even our understanding of Martian life (lower left corner) has changed as new discoveries are made.

A statue of Mars, the Roman god of war.

the planet was named Nergal in honor of the god of war and death. The ancient Greeks called the planet Ares after their god of war. The Romans gave the name Mars to the planet. Like the Greeks, the Romans identified the planet with blood, war, and violence. Today, many call Mars the "Red Planet."

BRAHE AND KEPLER

Tycho Brahe was a Danish astronomer who lived during the sixteenth century. Between 1576 and 1596, Brahe made a series of drawings that showed the movements of the planets. Mars especially interested him. Using only his eyes and various measuring instruments, he charted the movement of Mars over the course of a year.

Even without a telescope, Brahe still had one of the best observatories in the world. His assistant was a bright young German mathematician named Johannes Kepler. Like many astronomers of his time, Brahe thought that Earth was the center of the universe and all the planets revolved around it in perfect circles.

Kepler, however, disagreed. He thought that the Sun was the center, but could not prove it. Kepler eventually realized that the drawings of Mars in orbit clearly showed that the planet's orbit was not a perfect circle, but was an **ellipse**. Using these drawings as a starting point, Kepler proved that the old Earth-centered image of the Solar System was wrong. He showed that all the planets, including Earth, revolve around the Sun in elliptical orbits, not perfect circles. Kepler even figured out the distance between Mars and the Sun at different times during its orbit.

WILLIAM HERSCHEL

In 1757, Wilhelm Herschel left his home in Germany at the age of nineteen and began a musical career in England where he changed his name to William. In his mid-thirties, he happened to read a book on astronomy. This book changed his life and inspired him to become an astronomer. With the help of his scientist sister Caroline, he developed many telescopes that could see across very far distances.

From his telescopic observations, Herschel figured out that Mars was tilted on its axis by about 25 degrees. Since Earth's

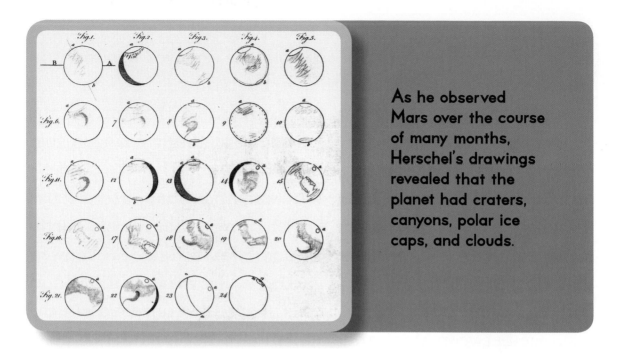

As he observed Mars over the course of many months, Herschel's drawings revealed that the planet had craters, canyons, polar ice caps, and clouds.

axial tilt is about the same, Herschel concluded that Mars must have seasons like our own. He also thought he observed clouds above the Martian surface. This led him to suspect that the planet had an Earth-like atmosphere. The Red Planet's bright polar regions reminded him of ice caps. He thought the planet's dark areas were probably seas, and the light orange areas were dry land. Herschel believed that since they lived on a planet so much like Earth, the Martians "probably enjoy a situation in many respects similar to ours."

SCHIAPARELLI'S CANALS

In 1877, the American astronomer Asaph Hall discovered the two moons of Mars, which he named Deimos and Phobos, which

CAROLINE HERSCHEL

Caroline Lucretia Herschel was William Herschel's younger sister. When Caroline eventually joined her brother in England, she became interested in mathematics and astronomy. In 1786 Caroline discovered her first comet. This discovery launched her career as a highly respected astronomer. By 1797, she had discovered eight more comets. In 1828 Caroline received the gold medal from England's Royal Astronomical Society for her many contributions to science.

meant "terror" and "fear." In September of the same year, Giovanni Schiaparelli, a respected Italian astronomer, made a detailed map of Mars. Over the next ten years, Schiaparelli kept adding more and more geographical features, giving them names from the Bible and other sources. His map stayed in use until the twentieth century, when more powerful telescopes could accurately view Mars. But his method of naming features on Mars is still used.

Schiaparelli also found what he thought was a network of criss-crossing lines on the surface of Mars. He called them "canali." In Italian the word *canali* can mean either human-made water

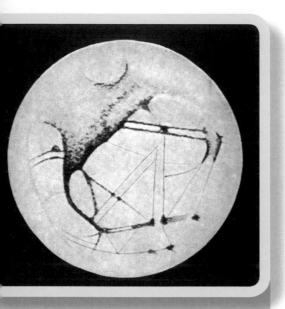

Published in 1890, this drawing by Schiaparelli shows the canali that he observed on the surface of Mars. Some scientists believed that these lines were proof that life-forms were making these "canals" on Mars.

channels or naturally formed river-beds. (*Canali* sounds very much like the English word canals.) Schiaparelli admitted that he did not really know what these lines were. Other scientists were more than willing to believe he had found Martian-made canals. As a result, the belief that Martian life existed became stronger.

MARTIANS

A great believer in the existence of Martian-made canals was nineteenth-century French astronomer Camille Flammarion. He had his own observatory near Paris. His writings about life on Mars had little scientific basis, but strongly appealed to the imaginations of his readers. In one of his books, he wrote, "Mars appears to be habitable to the same degree as the Earth. It is older, and so its humanity could be more advanced than ourselves . . . the climate and conditions for life on Mars appear to be similar enough to Earth that species slightly different from ours could live there."

Flammarion's ideas about intelligent life on Mars made him a very popular astronomer. But toward the end of the nineteenth century, an American astronomer named Percival Lowell outdid him in popularity. In 1894, Lowell opened a large observatory near Flagstaff, Arizona, and called it Mars Hill. Lowell and his assistants made drawings of what they saw through the telescope. After a year of observing Mars almost nightly, Lowell published a series of four articles and then a book based on these articles. Simply called *Mars*, his book made him famous overnight. People flocked to his lectures to hear his ideas about the history of Mars and what life was like on this planet.

According to Lowell, the Martian climate was warmer than Earth's. Mars had lost much of its atmosphere but could still support life. With very little rainfall, the planet had become mostly desert. In order to survive, Martians had learned to cooperate and to share limited natural resources. They built a series of canals to carry water from melting polar ice caps and irrigate the drier parts of the planet. Lowell thought that the dark green areas visible through a telescope were actually farmlands.

He believed that Martians were probably many times larger and stronger than people on Earth. Since Mars had much less gravity, the planet could easily handle larger forms of life. Lowell guessed that the average Martian was about 20 feet (6 meters) tall, had the strength of fifty humans, and would weigh about 4,000 pounds (1,816 kilograms) on Earth.

By the early 1900s, Percival Lowell was considered an expert on Mars and Martian civilization. But not everyone accepted his theories. Other astronomers tried to prove the existence of canals but were unable to see them, even when they used more powerful telescopes. A Martian canal controversy that began with Giovanni Schiaparelli once again flared up, this time between "canalists," or people who believed that Martians made the canals, and "anti-canalists" who doubted the canals and Martians' existence.

The canalists believed the crisscrossing lines on the Martian surface were proof of intelligent life. Only an advanced civilization, they argued, could have built such a complex system of canals for carrying snow melt from the Martian poles to the drier areas of the planet. The "anti-canalists," on the other hand, suspected that Lowell's eyes had been playing tricks on him.

An English astronomer in 1903 conducted an experiment with thirteen-year-old students to demonstrate how Lowell had been fooled. He showed the students a drawing containing smudges, squiggles, and spots, and asked them to draw what they saw. Students in the front, sitting closer to the drawings, drew random, unrelated shapes. But students in the back of the classroom automatically connected the shapes into straight lines. The lines looked a lot like Lowell's Martian canals. But even the results of this experiment failed to convince those who wanted to believe there really were canals on Mars.

THE MARTIANS HAVE LANDED!

While many scientists were beginning to doubt Lowell's ideas about Mars, the general public continued to believe that life would be found there. In 1898 the British writer H. G. Wells, inspired by Lowell's book *Mars*, published *War of the Worlds*, a science-fiction novel. In the book, technologically superior Martians invade Earth because their own planet is dying. Lowell had imagined Martians as peaceful, wise beings. But Wells turned them into hostile creatures bent on destroying human civilization. Wells' Martians easily conquered England but then were defeated by the one thing they have no defense against—germs, or sickness, found on Earth.

In 1938, the American actor and director Orson Welles and the Mercury Theatre on the Air broadcast their own version of the novel by H. G. Wells. The radio play aired on October 30, one day before Halloween. During the broadcast, Wells announced that what people were hearing on their radios was just a play and not real life. But these announcements did not stop people all over America from panicking. Many actually believed that Martians had landed in Grover's Mill, New Jersey, and were causing massive destruction. Frightened by what they took to be actual news reports, people warned their friends and neighbors, phoned loved ones to say goodbye, and sped off in their cars to escape the invaders from outer space.

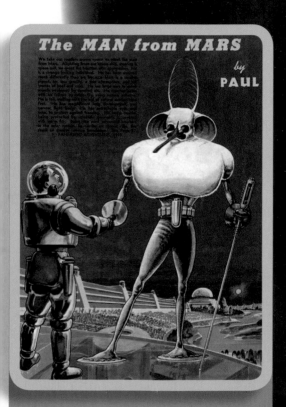

Not all stories portrayed Martians as cruel creatures eager to destroy humans. Some people believed that the aliens were curious and peaceful beings.

MARS AND MARINER SPACE PROGRAMS

Scientists generally agree that the space age began in 1957 with the launch of the Soviet **satellite** *Sputnik*. The purpose of this mission was to get a close-up look at Earth's Moon. In 1962 the Soviets launched *Mars 1*, the first attempt in human history to look at Mars from outer space instead of from Earth-based observatories.

The space **probe** *Mars 1* came within 120,000 miles (193,000 km) of Mars. It transmitted data for two years before finally quitting. Meanwhile, the United States embarked on its own series of unmanned missions to Mars. NASA's *Mariner* space program included nine separate missions. *Mariner 4* was the first successful mission. Launched on November 28, 1964, the vehicle was small by today's standards. It has been described as a "windmill hurtling through space." It weighed about 575 pounds (261 kg) and was about 9 feet (2.7 m) by 22 feet (6.7 m) in size.

No Signs of Life

On July 14, 1965, *Mariner 4* reached its destination, 228 days after its launch. It came within 6,114 miles (9,846 km) of Mars. A camera on board the vehicle transmitted the first close-up photographs of Mars ever taken. Many observers were deeply disappointed. They had hoped the photos would reveal signs of life or at least a life-supportive environment. Instead the photos showed a dry, dusty surface pockmarked with craters. There was no water anywhere to be seen. If anything, Mars had more in common with our moon than with Earth. Newspapers began referring to the Red Planet as "the dead planet."

Warm Daytime Temperatures

Mariner 6 and *Mariner 7* came even closer to Mars. Both probes passed within 2,175 miles (3,500 km) of the planet in the summer of 1969. The two probes sent back more than two hundred images of Mars. Again, there were no signs of canals or any forms of life. The great canal controversy appeared to be finally

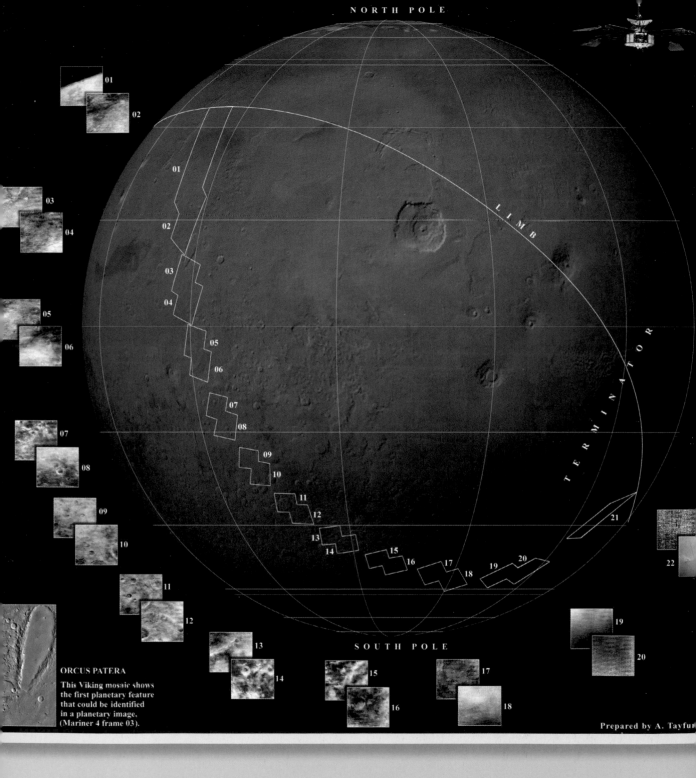

NORTH POLE

01
02

01

02

03
04

03

05
06

04

05

06

07
08

L I M B

07
08

T E R M I N A T O R

09
10

09
10

11
12

11
12

13
14

13
14

15
16

15

21

SOUTH POLE

17
18

17

19
20

20

22

19

ORCUS PATERA

This Viking mosaic shows
the first planetary feature
that could be identified
in a planetary image.
(Mariner 4 frame 03).

Prepared by A. Tayfur

The black and white images shown here are surface images taken by *Mariner 4.* (The
planetary image of Mars, which indicates where each *Mariner 4* photograph was
taken, comes from the *Viking* spacecraft.)

settled. However, *Mariner 6* and *Mariner 7* measured temperatures on Mars and discovered that daytime temperatures near the Martian equator could reach a high of 60 degrees Fahrenheit (16 degrees C). But at night the temperature dropped below -110 degrees Fahrenheit (-80 degrees C). Temperatures at the Martian poles were even colder, reaching -220 degrees Fahrenheit (-140 degrees C). The probes also determined that the polar caps were largely made of frozen carbon dioxide. On Earth this substance is known as dry ice and is used to keep things very cold.

While the Mariner space program was underway, the Soviet Union continued to launch its own Martian probes. Both *Mars 2* and *3* carried their own landers, which are spacecraft equipped to land on the surface of a planet. The lander aboard *Mars 2* was the first human-made object to penetrate the Martian atmosphere. Unfortunately, it crashed before it could send any data back to Earth. The *Mars 3* lander made a successful landing but then a violent dust storm prevented it from functioning.

Underground Ice and Breathtaking Landscapes

The next big breakthrough in the scientific exploration of Mars was NASA's *Mariner 9*. Launched on May 30, 1971, it took only 167 days to reach Mars. This unmanned probe became the first spacecraft to orbit another planet. Circling within 1,025 miles

Mariner 9 became the first probe to orbit a planet other than Earth. An artist's depiction of the orbit shows an enlarged view of Earth and the Moon just past Mars.

(1,650 km) of the surface, it took more than 7,300 photographs in the course of one year. More than any of the earlier probes, *Mariner 9* revealed the many faces of the Martian landscape. The photos showed enormous volcanoes, incredibly gigantic canyons, and areas of permafrost, which is ground that is permanently frozen. The permafrost alone was a major discovery. It suggested that Mars might contain water in the form of underground ice. Scientists guessed that if water is present on Mars, could there be some form of life, too? Even if no life currently exists on Mars, could the planet have supported life in the past?

Mariner 9's round-the-planet photos allowed astronomers to create the first detailed map of another planet in our Solar System. They also showed that the large dark green patches on the surface of Mars, once thought to be vegetation, are actually rocky areas that look green when seen through a telescope.

A Place Where Water Once Flowed

Mariner 9's most astonishing discovery was the evidence of dry riverbeds. Thousands of them marked the planet's surface. This could only mean one thing: in the very distant past, huge amounts of water must have flowed freely on Mars. Water and life go hand in hand. So it was reasonable for astronomers to think that plants and animals may have once thrived on Mars. But the planet would have needed a much thicker atmosphere and a much warmer climate in order for Mars to have so much water. Now the climate is too cold and dry, and the atmosphere is too thin. The information from *Mariner 9* gave rise to new questions about the Red Planet. Why did the Martian atmosphere become so thin? Why is the planet so much colder than Earth? And what happened to all that water?

TWO VIKINGS

The dramatic success of *Mariner 9* inspired NASA scientists to attempt to land a spacecraft on Mars and hunt for signs of life. The new mission involved a pair of spacecraft named *Viking 1* and *Viking 2*. Both spacecraft had an orbiter and a

This image was taken by one of the *Viking* orbiters in 1976, and shows some of the large and inactive volcanoes on the surface of Mars.

lander. Scientists carefully selected two different landing sites. On August 20, 1975, *Viking 1* was launched. It touched down on the Martian surface on July 20, almost one year later. *Viking 2*, launched in September 1975, landed the following September. Both vehicles landed intact and continued to perform until the early 1980s.

The two Viking missions pushed the exploration of Mars further than it had ever been before. Thanks to these missions, we now know why the Red Planet is so red. Rich deposits of iron in Martian rocks have rusted. We also learned why the Martian sky has its distinctive color. Dust storms on the planet's surface blast pink and red soil particles into the air.

Testing Soil Samples on Mars

These discoveries were only part of what the *Viking* missions accomplished. The orbiters mapped more than 97 percent of the planet and determined that the north polar cap contains water in the form of ice. The landers collected soil samples, studied climate changes, and measured wind speeds. Each lander had its own laboratory for analyzing the soil samples and looking for evidence of organic life, past or present.

The laboratories on the *Viking* landers ran a series of tests on the Martian soil. The tests found signs of chemical reactions but nothing that showed organic life was present. However, some of the scientists on the *Viking* mission teams doubted the results

THE FACE ON MARS AND OTHER STRANGE SIGHTS

Another controversy that grew out of the two Viking missions was related to the photographs of the Martian surface. One scientist, examining the photos, noticed a rock with what looked like the letter B. When reporters heard this, their imaginations went into high gear. Peering into NASA monitors in Pasadena, California, they soon began seeing more letters as well as numbers carved into Martian rocks.

Before long, television viewers were sure that Martians had carved these messages in order to communicate with us. People also claimed the photographs from Mars revealed even more evidence of Martian civilization. They saw pyramids, entire cities, and a giant human face in the images sent from Mars. Were their eyes playing tricks on them or had they really seen objects made by Martian hands?

NASA scientists explained that the markings were the result of natural processes. But many citizens remained doubtful. They believed the Viking missions had proved that Martians existed and that the government was covering up the evidence to keep people from panicking. In reality, no such evidence has been found.

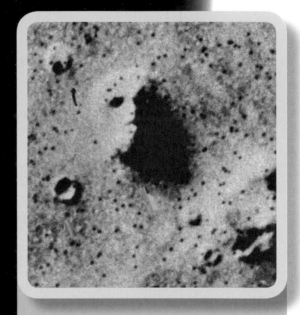

Scientists believe that the "face" on the surface of Mars is actually a combination of rocks and shadows.

of these tests. One of those scientists was Carl Sagan. He argued that living **microbes** in the soil might have caused the reactions that the experiments had detected. And even if microbes were not in the soil samples, maybe they would be found deep underground. Sagan also wondered if the fossilized remains of ancient plants and animals might also be buried underground.

If there was any kind of organic life on Mars, the only way to find out would be to bring soil samples back to Earth or send astronauts to Mars. With the failure of the *Viking* missions to find signs of life, scientific interest in the exploration of Mars began to fade. This changed when a greenish rock about the size of a potato, found by accident near Earth's South Pole, prompted a whole new set of questions and a second round of missions to Mars.

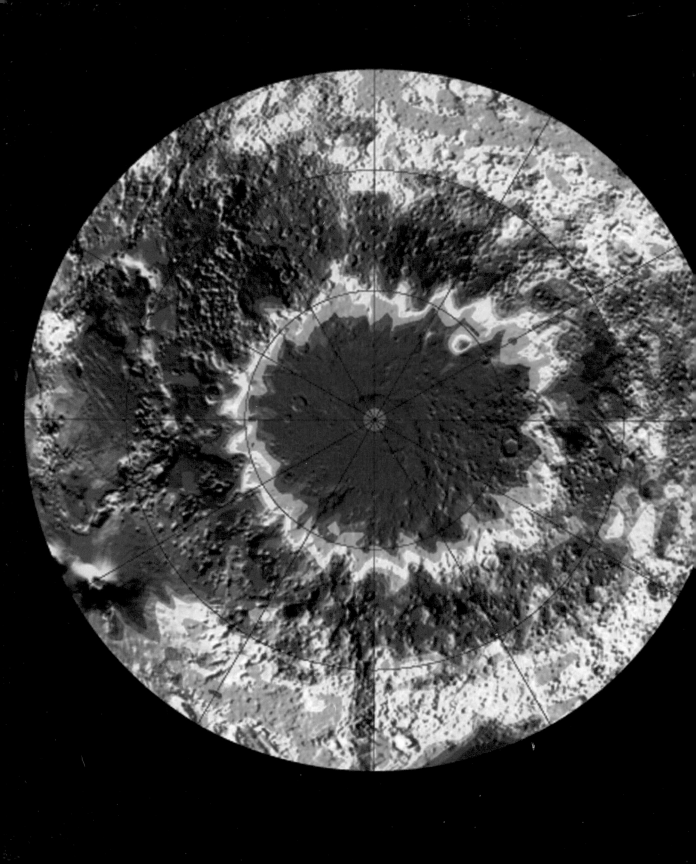

4

NEW QUESTIONS, NEW DISCOVERIES

Roberta Score, an American geologist, was snowmobiling with fellow scientists near the South Pole. The exact location was Alan Hills, and the year was 1984. Score noticed a green-colored rock in the ice. Something about the rock intrigued her, so she sent it to the Johnson Space Center in Houston, Texas, for analysis. Scientists in Houston named the rock ALH84001. "ALH" stands for Allan Hills, and "84" is the year when the rock was discovered. For nine years it sat in storage at the Space Center. Then in 1993, scientists carried out a detailed analysis of the small, green rock.

The 2001 *Mars Odyssey* provided this view of the planet's south pole. The different colors represent the various amounts of hydrogen found in the soil. Future Mars missions may give us more details about the planet's chemical makeup.

Much to everyone's surprise, the rock turned out to be from Mars. But what was it doing on Earth and how did it get here? Even more important, what did the rock reveal about the possibility of life on Mars? Scientists are pretty certain they have answers for the first two questions. But the third question— what does ALH84001 tell us about life on Mars—has started a major controversy within the scientific community.

The rock is roughly 4.5 billion years old. It formed around the same time that Mars was taking shape. Millions of years ago, an asteroid or a giant meteorite probably smacked into Mars. The impact sent tons of rocks hurtling skyward. The rocks traveled so fast they were able to escape the gravitational pull of Mars. Instead of falling back onto the planet's surface, they ended up in the ice-cold void of outer space.

For about 16 million years, the rock from Mars wandered aimlessly in the Solar System. Its wandering days ended about 13,000 years ago when it strayed too close to Earth. Our planet's gravitational field grabbed the rock and pulled it into Earth's atmosphere. The rock had become a meteor that eventually crashed somewhere

ALH84001

Scientists today continue to study ALH84001 to see if it really is proof that there was once—and may still be—life on Mars.

in Antarctica. Thousands of years later, Roberta Score found the rock, but its journey was not yet over. It still had a puzzling story to tell.

Scientists understand the origin of ALH84001. However, they are still not sure about what the rock reveals about life on Mars. A careful analysis using an electron microscope discovered what could be the fossilized remains of Martian bacteria. If this were really the case, then we would know for sure that Earth is not the only place where life occurs. We could also be reasonably certain that Mars once had an environment in which living organisms could develop. But for now, scientists disagree about what these microscopic structures are and how they formed. Are they the remains of once-living Martian microbes, or are they only tiny crystals embedded in the rock? Maybe they are not even from Mars at all. The structures could be Earth-born bacteria that found their way into the rock in Antarctica.

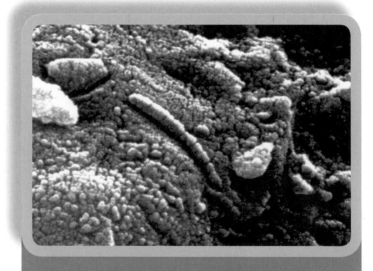

An image from an electron microscope scan shows what may be the remains of a tube-like organism from Mars.

This unsolved puzzle has sparked a controversy similar to the one between canalists and anti-canalists in the nineteenth and early twentieth centuries. Scientists who believe the microscopic, tube-shaped structures found in ALH84001 are the remains of Martian bacteria have been called "microfossilists." Those who believe otherwise are "anti-microfossilists." The structures themselves are so small it would take more than 250,000 of them, lined up end to end, to equal 1 inch (2.54 centimeters).

WHERE DID LIFE BEGIN?

Solving this puzzle could even open the door to a much larger understanding about the origin of life on Earth. In evolutionary theory, life on Earth began as single-celled organisms. During the course of millions of years, these simple organisms gradually evolved, becoming more and more complex. Eventually, they gave rise to the many kinds of species that now inhabit our world, from microbes to giant pandas and everything in between.

But what if Martian rocks landed on Earth millions of years ago and brought with them tiny microbes that began to grow and develop? What if all forms of life on Earth began with single-celled microbes from Mars? If that were true, then we humans are really Martians—at least in terms of our origins. On the other hand, it could be the other way around. What if an asteroid collided with Earth and propelled tons of rocks into space? Some of the rocks could have ended up on Mars. If they contained microscopic organisms, then the process of evolution might have begun there as well as on Earth. A third possibility is that seed-like **spores** blowing through space happened to land on both planets and began to grow and reproduce independently.

MARS GLOBAL SURVEYOR AND PATHFINDER

The discovery of the small, green rock near the South Pole led to a new interest in exploring Mars. Scientists hoped the next round of missions might finally answer the question of whether life currently exists on Mars or if it had existed there in the past. On November 6, 1996, the *Mars Global Surveyor* was launched. The spacecraft contained instruments for mapping the surface of Mars and for studying its atmosphere and polar ice caps. The mission goals were to create a detailed map of Mars, search for signs of life, and locate possible landing sites for future missions.

The *Mars Global Surveyor* did not land on Mars. After reaching the planet ten months after launch, it went into orbit. While it was in operation, the *Surveyor* completed twelve orbits a day and sent back images that were up to fifty times clearer than any previous images. These images gave scientists their most accurate view of the planet's environment.

This detailed image from the *Mars Global Surveyor* shows the walls of a meteor crater on Mars.

The *Surveyor* also tried to find out what happened to the planet's magnetic field. Most of the planets in our Solar System have what scientists call a magnetosphere, which is an invisible network of magnetic lines that trap charged particles. Venus and Mars do not appear to have such lines. Scientists want to know why. Instruments aboard the *Mars Global Surveyor* did find traces of magnetism below the Martian surface. But so far, the question of why the planet lacks a strong magnetic field remains unanswered.

Pathfinder

Pathfinder was launched one month after the *Mars Global Surveyor*. It reached speeds of 17,000 miles (27,400 km) per hour, covered more than 408,000 miles (658 km) a day, and slammed into the Martian atmosphere on July 4, 1997, two months before the *Surveyor*. Heat shields kept *Pathfinder* from burning up on entry. As *Pathfinder* approached the surface of Mars, three large parachutes opened, slowing down the lander's speed to about 35 miles (56 km) per hour. Then huge air bags inflated in just two seconds.

Pathfinder bounced about sixteen times before coming to rest. *Pathfinder* had landed on a rolling plain known as Ares Villis. Within minutes, *Pathfinder* began to communicate with NASA computers on Earth. It also lowered a ramp to the Martian surface. Out came *Sojourner*, the first rover ever to set wheels on another planet. It was about the size of a microwave oven, had six wheels, and could maneuver on its own using lasers to feel its way around and to avoid obstacles.

While instruments aboard the lander analyzed the atmosphere, *Sojourner* studied nearby rocks and soil. It detected large deposits of silicon. On Earth volcanic rocks typically contain silicon. So it is likely that Mars once had many active volcanoes.

Since the *Mariner 9* mission twenty-six years earlier, scientists had become very interested in understanding the role of water in the history of Mars. *Mariner 9* convinced scientists that liquid water had once flowed on Mars. Photographic images showed markings that resembled dry riverbeds on Earth. *Mariner 9* also detected ice in the polar caps of Mars and underground deposits of ice in the form of permafrost.

In 1997, *Pathfinder*'s rover gave scientists more evidence that water once flowed on Mars. Using the rover's roving "eye," they looked at the way rocks were laid out around the landing site.

Part of *Sojourner*'s mission was to analyze the chemicals that make up some of the planet's different rocks.

The rocks appeared to have been tumbled into place. The likely cause was a powerful river or flood. The body of water would have flowed through the Ares Villis plain and was possibly hundreds of miles wide!

In September 1997, NASA lost contact with the *Pathfinder*'s lander. Six months later, the mission officially ended. What about *Sojourner*? Since the little rover runs on solar power, it could still be roaming around, bumping into things. Then again, it might have stopped working years ago.

SPIRIT AND OPPORTUNITY

In 2003, NASA launched two new spacecraft destined for Mars. The launches were one month apart. The spacecraft landed in January 2004. Each one contained an advanced kind of rover. The rovers were called *Spirit* and *Opportunity*. Unlike *Pathfinder*'s rover, these improved models have been able to explore much more of the Martian terrain. They were only expected to last for about ninety days. But after four years, *Spirit* and *Opportunity* were still in operation. Much larger than *Sojourner*, the rovers each weigh about 400 pounds (180 kg). They carry identical sets of scientific instruments for probing their alien surroundings. Special scraping tools can scratch the surface of Martian rocks so scientists can study the rocks' interior.

The twin rovers have supplied a lot of information about Martian rocks and soils. They have also sent back more than 100,000 color images of the landscape and confirmed that water was once present. Thanks to the rovers' investigations, scientists are reasonably sure that millions of years ago Mars had a warmer climate and a thicker atmosphere. Under these conditions, ancient Martian rivers probably turned volcanic craters into lakes and created oceans in the lowland areas.

Many questions still remain. When did Mars have rivers, lakes, and oceans? How long did the planet have so much water? Where did all this water go? Why did the climate become so cold and dry? Of course, the really big question is did life develop on Mars? And if it did, what happened to it? We know that the total amount of bacteria on Earth is greater than the combined mass of all of Earth's plants and animals. That is a lot of microbes! Some forms of bacteria have been found in extremely harsh environments on Earth, such as Antarctica or deep in the ocean near heat vents. So it might be possible for microbes to live in harsh conditions on other planets.

So far no life has been found on Mars, where conditions are much harsher than anything here. But perhaps Martian bacteria live below the surface of the planet in warm, **geothermal** pools. They might have also become **dormant** in order to survive. Some scientists even wonder if Mars is going through its own Ice Age. If the planet ever warms up again, dormant bacteria might "wake up" even after millions of years have passed. Understanding climate change on Mars may even enable us to understand climate change on Earth.

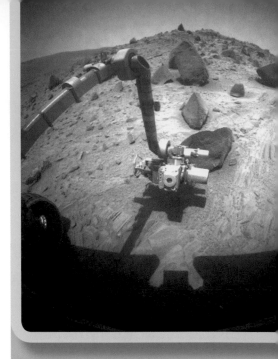

Rock samples examined by Mars rovers continue to give scientists a better idea of how Mars was formed.

MANNED MISSIONS AND BEYOND

Sending astronauts to Mars will likely be the next major step in the exploration of this planet. But manned missions will not happen for at least another twenty-five years or so. That is how long it will take to design and test new rockets, spacesuits, and life-support systems. Space expeditions also cost a lot of money, and it will take a while to come up with enough money to cover the very high cost of these experiments.

NASA officials are committed to eventually putting humans on Mars, but the first step will be putting astronauts on the Moon. The last time an astronaut set foot on the Moon was more than thirty years ago. The visit was a short one—about one day. But the next generation of astronauts might actually live on the Moon for longer periods of time. They will experience what it is like to live and work in an environment with one-sixth of Earth's gravity. They will also test new kinds of spacesuits designed to protect space travelers from Mars' solar radiation, low atmospheric pressure, and extremely cold climate. In addition, for the first time in human history they will know what it is like to live on a Solar System body other than our own.

Future lunar, or Moon, expeditions will give scientists vital information they need to help astronauts survive a mission to Mars. The trip to Mars will take many months and will cover millions of miles in space. Once there, astronauts will have to stay for about one-and-a-half years until Mars comes closest to Earth again. When that happens, the journey home will be much faster than at other times.

A major reason for sending people to Mars is to look for signs of past or present life. Manned missions may finally give us the answer to a very big question: Is life something rare in the universe or is it commonplace, happening on many worlds

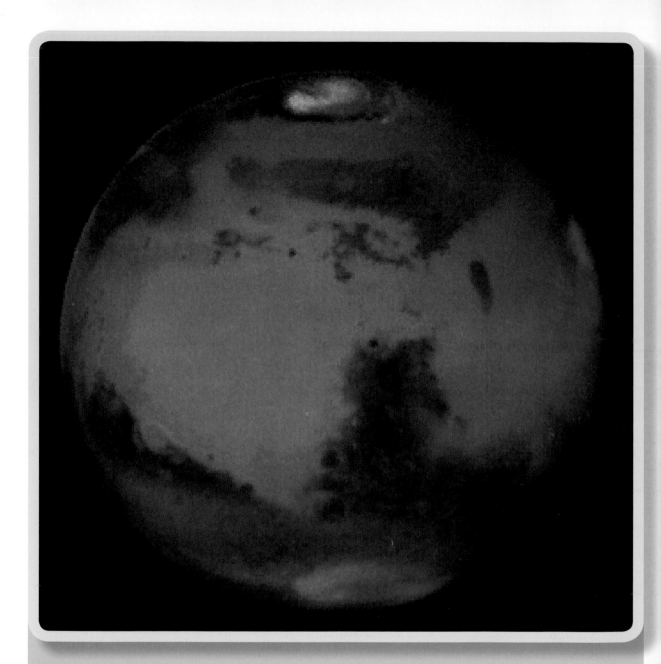

Scientists continue to gather as much evidence as they can to better understand the structure and environment of the Red Planet. This may lead to a better understanding of how the planet can support life.

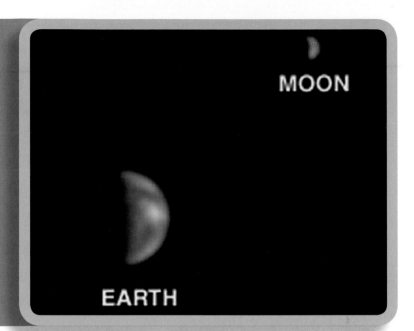

This colorized photograph shows what Earth and the Moon look like from Mars. Perhaps someday humans will be able to colonize the Red Planet, and this is the view they will see when they gaze into the Martian sky.

and not just on our own? A related question is whether Mars will be able to sustain life in the future. It is possible that one day Mars will be our second home—a place where humans will pass their entire lives without ever setting foot on Earth.

MARS: THE NEXT EARTH?

Looking beyond manned flights to Mars, some scientists and science fiction writers imagine a time when people will colonize the planet. For this to happen, Mars will have to go through a major makeover. As things stand now, Mars is not livable. Freezing temperatures, dust storms that can sweep across the entire planet, no surface water, and deadly ultraviolet radiation are some of the dangers that would make living on Mars just about impossible.

So what would it take for humans to find Mars a reasonable place to live? One idea is to terraform the planet. The astronomer Carl Sagan figured it would take thousand of years to terraform Mars. Such an undertaking would involve making Mars as Earth-like as possible, with plenty of water, a moderate climate, good farmland, and a thicker breathable atmosphere. But how can people do this? One scientist has proposed surrounding Mars with giant mirrors hung in space. The mirrors would reflect sunlight toward the polar ice caps. The sunlight would then melt the ice, giving Mars a steady supply of running water. Another idea is to build factories on Mars that would produce nothing but greenhouse gases. These gases would trap sunlight, heating up the atmosphere so underground ice would melt and rise to the surface.

Carl Sagan even thought it would be a good idea to construct canals to carry water from the melting ice caps to the drier parts of the planet. If that were happen, then the canalists who believed Martians built canals on Mars would be proven right after all. Only the Martians would be us and the canals would be the work of our own hands.

QUICK FACTS ABOUT MARS

NAME AND ORIGIN OR SOURCE OF NAME: Mars, Roman god of war

NICKNAME: The Red Planet

SIZE: About 4,128 miles (6,792 km) in diameter

DISTANCE FROM EARTH: About 142 million miles (228 million km), but may vary since Mars has an elliptical orbit

DISTANCE FROM THE SUN: About 142 million miles (228 million km), but varies from 36 million miles (58 million km) to more than 250 million miles (402 million km) since Mars has an elliptical orbit

NUMBER OF MOONS: Two—Phobos and Deimos

TYPE OF PLANET: Terrestrial

TEMPERTAURE RANGE: -220 degrees Fahrenheit (-140 degrees C) to 50 degrees Fahrenheit (10 degrees C)

LENGTH OF DAY: 24 hours, 37 minutes

LENGTH OF YEAR: 686.98 Earth days (about 670 Mars days)

MISSIONS TO MARS: Flybys: *Mariners 4, 6,* and *7;* Orbiters: *Mariner 9, Vikings 1* and *2, Mars Global Surveyor, 2001 Mars Odyssey.* Landed missions: *Vikings 1* and *2, Pathfinder, Spirit, Opportunity*

GLOSSARY

astronomers—Scientists who study planets, stars, and galaxies.

atmosphere— All the gases that surround a planet or a star.

atom—The basic building block of all matter.

axis—An imaginary straight line going through the center of a planet around which the planet or other celestial body rotates. The axis of Earth and Mars are tipped at about the same angle.

dormant—Not actively growing or showing signs of life, but capable of becoming active again.

ellipse—An oval shaped like a slightly flattened circle.

geothermal—Relating to sources of heat inside a planet like Earth or Mars.

mantle—An interior section of a planet that is located between the core and the outer crust.

microbe—A germ or other extremely small organism that can only be seen with a microscope.

molten—To be in liquid form as a result of intense heat.

probe—Any kind of spacecraft designed to explore extraterrestrial objects and send back data to computers on Earth.

satellite—Any natural or human-made object that orbits a larger body such as a planet or moon. The Moon is a satellite of Earth. The *Mars Global Surveyor*, which orbited Mars, is also a satellite. Human-made satellites transmit scientific data.

spores—Small, usually one-celled structures produced by seedless plants and some bacteria. In a harsh environment, spores can remain dormant for long periods of time. When conditions improve, they can develop into complete individuals of their species.

terrestrial—Relating to the land rather than the sea or atmosphere. Terrestrial planets like Mars and Earth have a solid surface made of rock and soil.

FIND OUT MORE

BOOKS

Bell, Jim. *Postcards from Mars: The First Photographer on the Red Planet*. New York: Penguin, 2006.

Goss, Tim. *Mars*. Chicago: Heinemann Library, 2008.

Irvine, Mat and David Jefferis. *Exploring Planet Mars*. New York: Crabtree Publishing: 2007.

Jefferis, David. *Mars: Distant Red Planet*. New York: Crabtree Publishing, 2008.

Miller, Ron. *Mars*. Brookfield, CT: Twenty-First Century Books, 2006.

Scott, Elaine. *Mars and the Search for Life*. New York: Clarion Books, 2008.

WEBSITES

Ask an Astronomer—Mars
http://coolcosmos.ipac.caltech.edu/cosmic_kids/AskKids/mars.shtml

Mars Express—European Space Agency
http://www.esa.int/SPECIALS/Mars_Express/index.html

Imagine Mars
http://imaginemars.jpl.nasa.gov/index2.html

Is There Life on Mars?
http://magma.nationalgeographic.com/ngexplorer/0401/articles/mainarticle.html

Mars
http://kids.nineplanets.org/mars.htm

Mars Exploration—Fun Zone!
http://marsprogram.jpl.nasa.gov/funzone_flash.html

Mission to Mars
http://athena.cornell.edu/kids

NASA Mars Exploration Program
http://mars.jpl.nasa.gov

NASA Solar System Exploration for Kids
http://solarsystem.nasa.gov/kids/index.cfm

Windows to the Universe—Mars
http://www.windows.ucar.edu/tour/link=/mars/mars.html

BIBLIOGRAPHY

The author found these resources especially helpful when researching this book.

Boyce, Joseph M. *The Smithsonian Book of Mars.* Washington and London: Smithsonian Institution Press, 2002.

CBS News. "The Next Giant Leap for Mankind." http://www.cbsnews.com/stories/2008/04/04/60minutes/main3994925.shtml

Miller, Ron and William K. Hartmann. *Grand Tour: A Traveler's Guide to the Solar System.* New York: Workman, 2005.

Moore, Patrick. *Patrick Moore on Mars.* London: Cassell, 1998.

NASA Mars Exploration Missions. http://mars.jpl.nasa.gov/missions/present/2003.html

NASA Mars Exploration Program. http://mars.jpl.nasa.gov/gallery/images.html

NASA Mars Global Surveyor. http://mgs-mager.gsfc.nasa.gov/Kids/funfacts.html

National Geographic. "Mars Colonies Coming Soon?" http://news.nationalgeographic.com/news/2005/03/0315_050315_marscolony.html

Raeburn, Paul. *Uncovering the Secrets of the Red Planet.* Washington, DC: National Geographic Society, 1998.

INDEX

ABOUT THE AUTHOR

George Capaccio is both a writer and a storyteller. He loves to visit schools and perform stories from all over the world for young audiences. He also enjoys writing educational books about history and science. He lives in Arlington, Massachusetts, with his wife, Nancy, and their Golden Retriever.